P9-DMA-863

A Special Gift

Presented to:

_____

From:

_____

Date:

_____

A Lasting Heritage for Your Children

A Father's Legacy

Your Life Story in Your Own Words

COUNTRYMAN®

NASHVILLE

A Thomas Nelson Company

Contents

Introduction

· · · · · · · · · · · · · · · · · ·

"What grade did you get in high school English, Dad?"
"What did you do on your first date?" Sound familiar?
Your son or daughter has probably asked these questions
and many more. Why? Curiosity partly, but mostly
because they care—about you. They want to know what
you did when you were growing up because they want to
know you.

That is the purpose of this book, which is a book about
you—your family history, your childhood memories,
humorous incidents, and meaningful traditions from your
life. It is a personal biography just waiting to be written.
Yes, there are planes to catch, meetings to attend, grass to
mow, and the car to wash, but those are not a legacy you
can pass on to your child. This book is.

Presented in a twelve-month format, this journal provides
an array of questions your son or daughter might ask
with space for your answers. Questions like, "Describe
the most fun you ever had on a Fourth of July."

Or "When you went to a ball game as a boy, what kind of food did you eat?" Or "What is the nicest thing you ever did for your mother and father?"

These questions will help you write down the special memories, thoughts, and ideas you want to share with your children. You may choose to complete the journal in a few days, a few weeks, or throughout the course of the year. When you have filled in all of the pages you will have a loving memoir—a spiritual legacy—to pass on to your children. They will cherish this book about you for a lifetime.

This book is for fathers of all ages, because it is never too early or too late to share your life with those you love. May *A Father's Legacy* draw you closer to your children as you share this memoir of your life…straight from your heart to theirs.

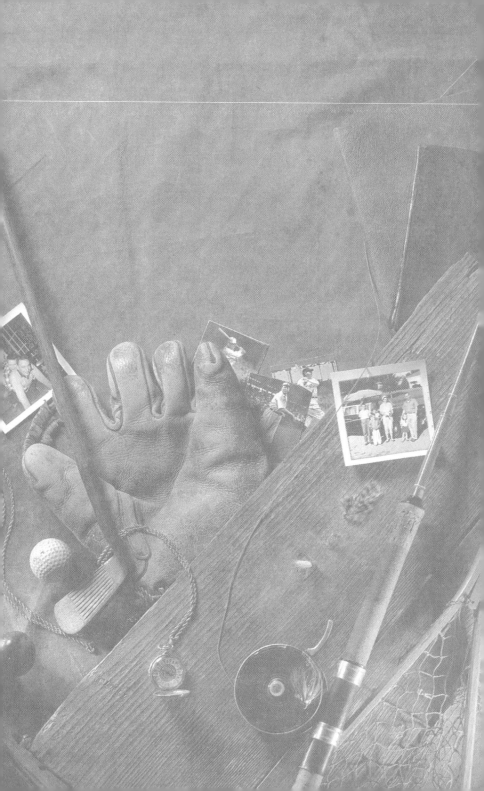

January

Our stories are
inextricably interwoven.
What you do is part of my story;
what I do is part of yours.

DANIEL TAYLOR

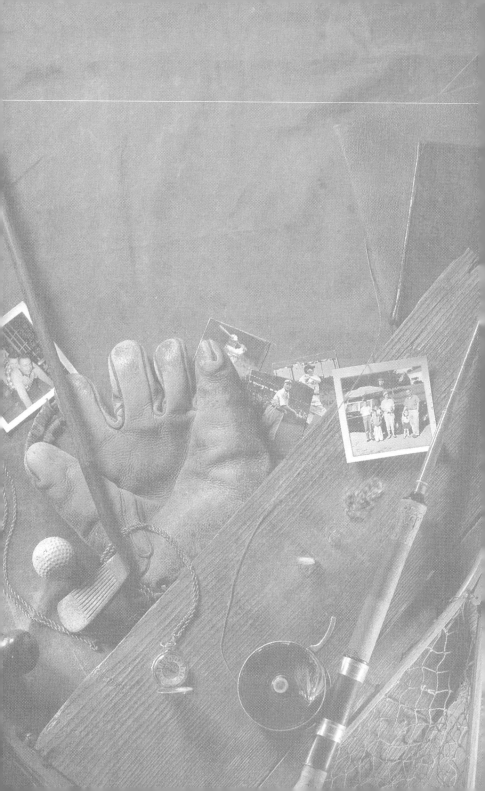

What did you enjoy doing most as a child?
*Did you prefer doing it alone or with someone else?*___

_____
_____
_____
_____
_____
_____
_____
_____
_____
_____
_____
_____
_____
_____
_____
_____
_____
_____
_____
_____
_____
_____
_____
_____
_____

—January—

W ho gave you your name and why?
Did you have a nickname? How did you get it? _____

_____
_____
_____
_____
_____
_____
_____
_____
_____
_____
_____
_____
_____
_____
_____
_____
_____
_____
_____
_____
_____
_____
_____
_____
_____

Describe your childhood home.
What was your favorite room?

_____
_____
_____
_____
_____
_____
_____
_____
_____
_____
_____
_____
_____
_____
_____
_____
_____
_____
_____
_____
_____
_____
_____
_____
_____
_____
_____
_____

Were you baptized or dedicated as an infant? If so, where and by whom? _____

_____

_____

_____

_____

_____

_____

_____

_____

_____

_____

_____

_____

_____

_____

_____

_____

_____

_____

_____

_____

_____

_____

_____

_____

_____

_____

_____

*D*id you attend church as a young boy?
What are your earliest memories of church? _____

_____

_____

_____

_____

_____

_____

_____

_____

_____

_____

_____

_____

_____

_____

_____

_____

_____

_____

_____

_____

_____

_____

_____

_____

_____

Where did your father go to work every day and what did he do? Did his work interest you?

_____
_____
_____
_____
_____
_____
_____
_____
_____
_____
_____
_____
_____
_____
_____
_____
_____
_____
_____
_____
_____
_____
_____
_____
_____
_____

Did your mother have a job or did she work at home?

_____

*What was your favorite sport or outdoor activity? Why was this your favorite?*_____

_____

_____

_____

_____

_____

_____

_____

_____

_____

_____

_____

_____

_____

_____

_____

_____

_____

_____

_____

_____

_____

Did you pray as a young boy?
If so, can you remember a specific prayer?
Who taught you to pray? _____.

_____
_____
_____
_____
_____
_____
_____
_____
_____
_____
_____
_____
_____
_____
_____
_____
_____
_____
_____
_____
_____
_____
_____
_____
_____
_____
_____

*W*here was your childhood home located?
Did you enjoy living there? _____

_____
_____
_____
_____
_____
_____
_____
_____
_____
_____
_____
_____
_____
_____
_____
_____
_____
_____
_____
_____
_____
_____
_____
_____

Describe your grandparents. What did you enjoy most about them?

Can you remember being afraid as a boy?
What was your greatest fear?
How did you deal with it? _____.

_____
_____
_____
_____
_____
_____
_____
_____
_____
_____
_____
_____
_____
_____
_____
_____
_____
_____
_____
_____
_____
_____
_____

Recall for me five
of the most important lessons
you have learned in life.

_____
_____
_____
_____
_____
_____
_____
_____
_____
_____
_____
_____
_____
_____
_____
_____
_____
_____
_____
_____

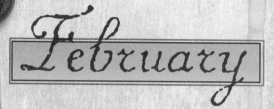

February

Gratitude is the
memory of the heart.

—•✦•—

MASSIEU

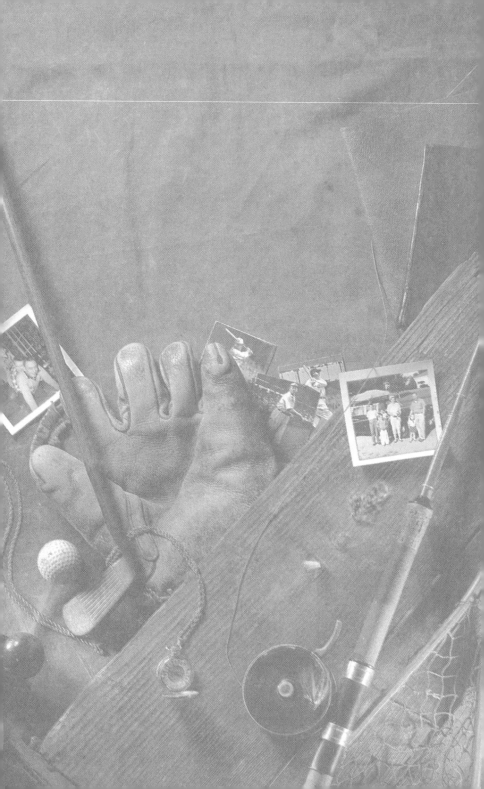

Did the pastor or a visiting
missionary ever eat dinner at your house?
Did they have an impact on your life?_____ .

_____ .
_____ .
_____ .
_____ .
_____ .
_____ .
_____ .
_____ .
_____ .
_____ .
_____ .
_____ .
_____ .
_____ .
_____ .
_____ .
_____ .
_____ .
_____ .
_____ .
_____ .
_____ .
_____ .

—February—

Did you ever feel that
God had a special calling on your life? _____

_____

_____

_____

_____

_____

_____

_____

_____

_____

_____

_____

_____

_____

_____

_____

_____

_____

_____

_____

_____

_____

_____

_____

_____

Describe the most memorable
Valentine you ever received.
Who sent it to you? _____

_____
_____
_____
_____
_____
_____
_____
_____
_____
_____
_____
_____
_____
_____
_____
_____
_____
_____
_____
_____
_____
_____
_____
_____

How far did you have to travel to attend elementary, junior high, and high school, and how did you get there? _____ .

_____

_____

_____

_____

_____

_____

_____

_____

_____

_____

_____

_____

_____

_____

_____

_____

_____

_____

_____

_____

_____

_____

_____

_____

_____

_____

_____

*W*ho gave you your first Bible
and how old where you when you received it.
How did it influence your life? _____

_____
_____
_____
_____
_____
_____
_____
_____
_____
_____
_____
_____
_____
_____
_____
_____
_____
_____
_____
_____
_____
_____
_____
_____

When did you become a Christian? How did your life change? _____

_____
_____
_____
_____
_____
_____
_____
_____
_____
_____
_____
_____
_____
_____
_____
_____
_____
_____
_____
_____
_____
_____
_____

Share your idea of
what makes a good friend.

_____
_____
_____
_____
_____
_____
_____
_____
_____
_____
_____
_____
_____
_____
_____
_____
_____
_____
_____
_____
_____

March

We have one life to live —
and one chance to live it in the
richest way possible.

JUDITH THURMAN

— *March* —

*D*o you remember your first communion?
What influence did it have on you and your family? _____

_____
_____
_____
_____
_____
_____
_____
_____
_____
_____
_____
_____
_____
_____
_____
_____
_____
_____
_____
_____
_____
_____
_____
_____
_____
_____

Describe your favorite
pastime or hobby as a child. _____
_____
_____
_____
_____
_____
_____
_____
_____
_____
_____
_____
_____
_____
_____
_____
_____
_____
_____
_____
_____
_____
_____
_____
_____
_____
_____

What mischievous prank did you pull on someone? How did it affect you?

_____
_____
_____
_____
_____
_____
_____
_____
_____
_____
_____
_____
_____
_____
_____
_____
_____
_____
_____
_____
_____
_____
_____
_____
_____
_____
_____

—*March*—

Did you have a television when you were growing up? What was your favorite program? Why? _____

_____

_____

_____

_____

_____

_____

_____

_____

_____

_____

_____

_____

_____

_____

_____

_____

_____

_____

_____

_____

_____

48

—*March*—

What were some crazy fads from your school days? Did you participate in them? Why or why not?

Who was your favorite teacher? How did that teacher influence your life?

— *March*—

Did you ever have a special hideaway or clubhouse? Describe it for me.

*In high school, what extracurricular
activities did you enjoy most?
Why did you choose those activities?* _____ .

_____
_____
_____
_____
_____
_____
_____
_____
_____
_____
_____
_____
_____
_____
_____
_____
_____
_____
_____
_____
_____
_____
_____

—*March*—

What is the nicest thing you ever did for your mother and father?

53

*D*id you admire a famous person?
What made that person admirable?

When did you have your first date? Tell me about it.

What do you remember about your first kiss?

_____
_____
_____
_____
_____
_____
_____
_____
_____
_____
_____
_____
_____
_____
_____
_____
_____
_____
_____
_____
_____
_____
_____
_____
_____
_____
_____

Share some of
your insights for working
well with others.

_____

_____

_____

_____

_____

_____

_____

_____

_____

_____

_____

_____

_____

_____

_____

_____

_____

_____

_____

JOE DI MAGGIO
outfield

BABE RUTH
pitcher—outfielder

TY COBB
outfield

April

$\mathcal{I}$t is in the shelter

of each other that the people live.

IRISH PROVERB

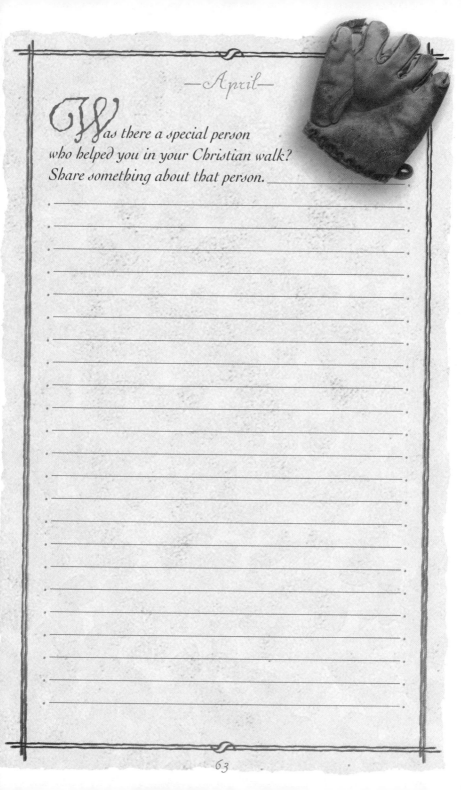

*W*as there a special person
who helped you in your Christian walk?
Share something about that person. _____

_____

_____

_____

_____

_____

_____

_____

_____

_____

_____

_____

_____

_____

_____

_____

_____

_____

_____

_____

_____

_____

_____

_____

_____

_____

—April—

W

hen did you first learn about sex?
Would you recommend the same for young people today?
Why or why not? _____

_____
_____
_____
_____
_____
_____
_____
_____
_____
_____
_____
_____
_____
_____
_____
_____
_____
_____
_____
_____
_____
_____
_____
_____
_____

—*April*—

*W*hat did your family like to do on week-
ends? Describe one particularly memorable one.

_____
_____
_____
_____
_____
_____
_____
_____
_____
_____
_____
_____
_____
_____
_____
_____
_____
_____
_____
_____
_____
_____
_____
_____
_____
_____

—April—

During childhood, who was your best friend?
Share some of your fondest memories of fun times together.

_____

_____

_____

_____

_____

_____

_____

_____

_____

_____

_____

_____

_____

_____

_____

_____

_____

_____

_____

_____

_____

_____

_____

_____

—April—

*D*id you ever keep a scrapbook of photos,
autographs, or memories of special occasions?
Describe what this meant to you. _____.

_____
_____
_____
_____
_____
_____
_____
_____
_____
_____
_____
_____
_____
_____
_____
_____
_____
_____
_____
_____
_____
_____
_____

—April—

What is your favorite memory of your mother? Why is it so special to you? _____

_____
_____
_____
_____
_____
_____
_____
_____
_____
_____
_____
_____
_____
_____
_____
_____
_____
_____
_____
_____
_____
_____
_____

Share with me your
father's attitude toward life
and how that affected you.

_____

_____

_____

_____

_____

_____

_____

_____

_____

_____

_____

_____

_____

_____

_____

_____

_____

_____

May

Who, being loved, is poor?

—❦—

OSCAR WILDE

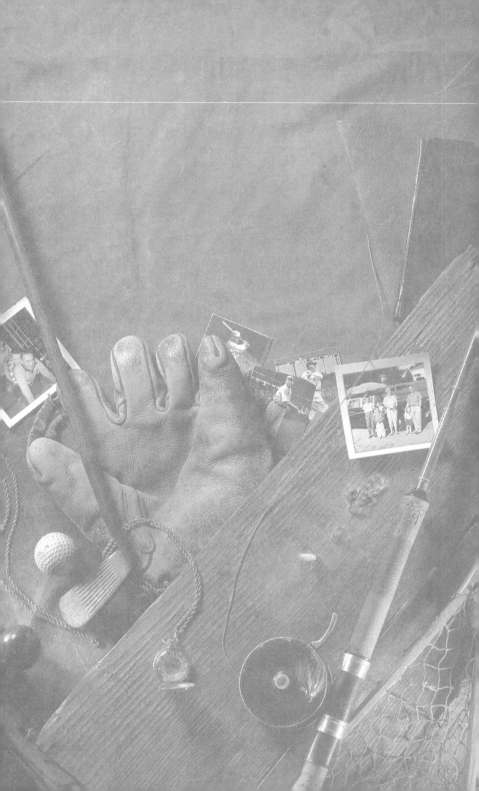

If you were to find an old toy box in your attic, what toys would you remember most fondly? Why?

_____
_____
_____
_____
_____
_____
_____
_____
_____
_____
_____
_____
_____
_____
_____
_____
_____
_____
_____
_____
_____
_____
_____
_____
_____
_____

How old were you when you understood
that God loves you? How did that affect your life?

—*May*—

*D*id *your family attend family reunions?*
What activities did everyone enjoy? Tell me about
your favorite cousins, aunts, or uncles. _____

_____
_____
_____
_____
_____
_____
_____
_____
_____
_____
_____
_____
_____
_____
_____
_____
_____
_____
_____
_____
_____
_____
_____
_____
_____

When you were young, did you
ever go to a funeral? How did that affect you.

_____
_____
_____
_____
_____
_____
_____
_____
_____
_____
_____
_____
_____
_____
_____
_____
_____
_____
_____
_____
_____
_____
_____
_____

If you had brothers and sisters,
did you feel your parents treated you all the same?
Why or why not? If you were an only child,
did you wish for brothers and sisters? Why? _____ .

_____
_____
_____
_____
_____
_____
_____
_____
_____
_____
_____
_____
_____
_____
_____
_____
_____
_____
_____
_____
_____
_____
_____
_____
_____

—*May*—

Did your high school have college or career days?
What field interested you most?
What did you want to become when you grew up? _____ .

_____
_____
_____
_____
_____
_____
_____
_____
_____
_____
_____
_____
_____
_____
_____
_____
_____
_____
_____
_____
_____
_____
_____

Share some principles from
Scripture on which you have
chosen to build your life.

_____

_____

_____

_____

_____

_____

_____

_____

_____

_____

_____

_____

_____

_____

_____

_____

_____

_____

June

The linking of generations,

the historical lineage of family,

the sharing of love . . .

give purpose to life.

GEORGE LANDBERG

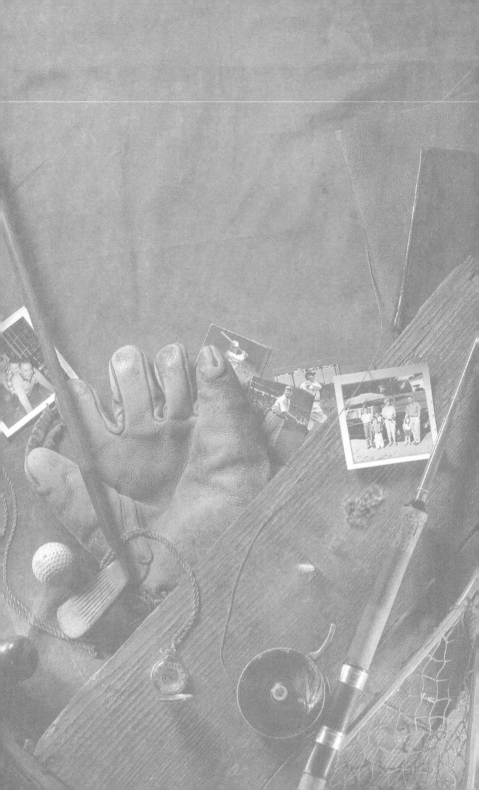

*I*f you learned to play a musical instrument, tell me
your memories of lessons, practice, and your music teacher.
If not, what instrument did you want to play and why?

_____

_____

_____

_____

_____

_____

_____

_____

_____

_____

_____

_____

_____

_____

_____

_____

_____

_____

_____

_____

_____

_____

_____

What were your youthful goals and ambitions for life? Which ones have you been able to fulfill?

How old were you when you met Mom? What attracted you to her?

—June—

When did you know that Mom was the "one and only one" for you? How did you know? _____

_____
_____
_____
_____
_____
_____
_____
_____
_____
_____
_____
_____
_____
_____
_____
_____
_____
_____
_____
_____
_____
_____
_____

—*June*—

$\mathcal{S}$hare a memory about the
way you proposed to Mom. _____

_____
_____
_____
_____
_____
_____
_____
_____
_____
_____
_____
_____
_____
_____
_____
_____
_____
_____
_____
_____
_____
_____
_____
_____
_____

Tell me about your wedding day.
What happened? How did you feel?
Were you nervous, scared, happy? _____

_____
_____
_____
_____
_____
_____
_____
_____
_____
_____
_____
_____
_____
_____
_____
_____
_____
_____
_____
_____
_____
_____
_____
_____
_____

—*June*—

Describe where you and Mom
lived after you got married. What was the
view like from the kitchen window? _____

_____
_____
_____
_____
_____
_____
_____
_____
_____
_____
_____
_____
_____
_____
_____
_____
_____
_____
_____
_____
_____
_____

When did you and Mom start talking about having children? Why did you want children —or did you?

_____

_____

_____

_____

_____

_____

_____

_____

_____

_____

_____

_____

_____

_____

_____

_____

_____

_____

_____

_____

_____

_____

_____

_____

_____

—June—

If you could go anywhere in the world on a second honeymoon, where would you go? Why?

—*June*—

What do you love best about Mom now?

_____
_____
_____
_____
_____
_____
_____
_____
_____
_____
_____
_____
_____
_____
_____
_____
_____
_____
_____
_____
_____
_____
_____
_____
_____
_____
_____

Record here your ideas on what it takes for a husband and wife to maintain a healthy marriage.

_____
_____
_____
_____
_____
_____
_____
_____
_____
_____
_____
_____
_____
_____
_____
_____
_____
_____
_____
_____
_____

July

Somehow, year after year,
Dad managed to take us on vacations
he couldn't afford to provide, in order
to make memories that we couldn't
afford to be without.

—

RICHARD EXLEY

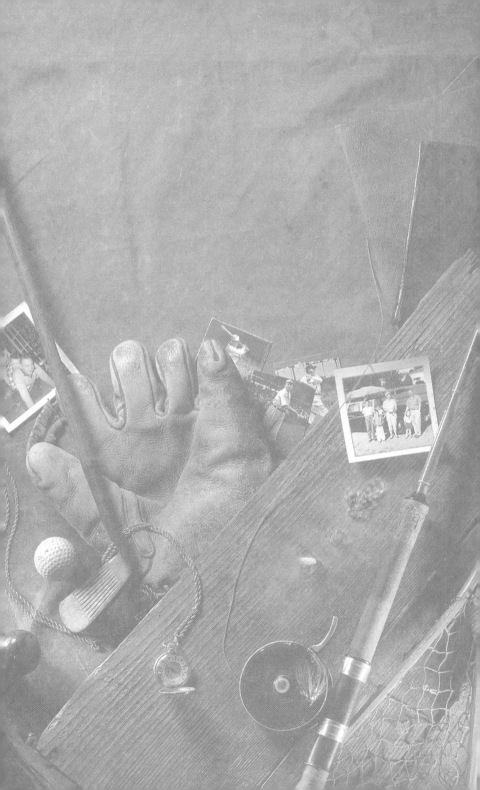

—July—

*If you served in the armed forces,
describe how your time in the service affected your life.
If you did not serve, how did this affect your life?* _____

_____
_____
_____
_____
_____
_____
_____
_____
_____
_____
_____
_____
_____
_____
_____
_____
_____
_____
_____
_____
_____
_____
_____
_____
_____
_____

*H*ave you ever believed so strongly in a cause
that you marched in a rally or demonstrated in protest?
What was the cause? Why was it important to you? _____

_____
_____
_____
_____
_____
_____
_____
_____
_____
_____
_____
_____
_____
_____
_____
_____
_____
_____
_____
_____
_____
_____

*W*hat is the gutsiest thing you
ever did in your life? Why did you do it?

*Where do you stand politically? Do you lean toward the left or the right? Who, if anyone, has most greatly influenced your current political views?*_____.

_____
_____
_____
_____
_____
_____
_____
_____
_____
_____
_____
_____
_____
_____
_____
_____
_____
_____
_____
_____
_____
_____
_____
_____
_____
_____

—*July*—

*D*id a tragedy ever strike your family?
If so, how did it affect you? _____

_____

_____

_____

_____

_____

_____

_____

_____

_____

_____

_____

_____

_____

_____

_____

_____

_____

_____

_____

_____

_____

_____

_____

_____

_____

_____

—July—

*W*hat is the best movie you've ever seen?
*If you could play one of the characters in the film,
whom would you choose, and why?*_____ .

_____ .
_____
_____ .
_____
_____ .
_____
_____ .
_____
_____ .
_____
_____ .
_____
_____ .
_____
_____ .
_____
_____ .
_____
_____ .
_____
_____ .
_____
_____ .
_____
_____ .
_____
_____ .
_____
_____ .
_____

*H*ow would you finish
this sentence? "One thing my
dad always said was . . ."

—July—

Did you ever go to summer camp?
Camping with the Boy Scouts?
Share one unforgettable memory. _____

_____
_____
_____
_____
_____
_____
_____
_____
_____
_____
_____
_____
_____
_____
_____
_____
_____
_____
_____
_____
_____
_____
_____
_____

Share a favorite poem,
passage of writing, or some
quotes that have been especially
meaningful in your life.

_____

_____

_____

_____

_____

_____

_____

_____

_____

_____

_____

_____

_____

_____

_____

_____

_____

_____

_____

_____

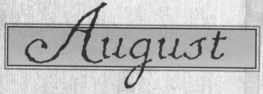

August

*W*hen I come home

from work and see those little noses

pressed against the window pane,

then I know I am a success.

PAUL FAULKNER

—*August*—

*I*s there any one book or author who helped you to develop a philosophy of life? Share some of those insights.

_____

_____

_____

_____

_____

_____

_____

_____

_____

_____

_____

_____

_____

_____

_____

_____

_____

_____

_____

_____

_____

_____

_____

—*August*—

*H*ow have your ideas about
God changed from when you were young?

What kind of outdoor work do you enjoy? Dislike?

—August—

What is your favorite way to spend a day of leisure?

_____

_____
_____
_____
_____
_____
_____
_____
_____
_____
_____
_____
_____
_____
_____
_____
_____
_____
_____
_____
_____
_____
_____
_____
_____
_____
_____
_____
_____

—*August*—

When did you learn how to ride a bike, or to water ski, snow ski, roller skate, or sail? Share your memories of the experience. _____.

_____
_____
_____
_____
_____
_____
_____
_____
_____
_____
_____
_____
_____
_____
_____
_____
_____
_____
_____
_____
_____
_____
_____
_____
_____
_____
_____

—*August*—

*Did you ever milk a cow or spend time
on a farm or in the country? Tell me about it.*

_____

_____

_____

_____

_____

_____

_____

_____

_____

_____

_____

_____

_____

_____

_____

_____

_____

_____

_____

_____

_____

_____

_____

_____

—*August*—

What places in the world would you still like to visit? Why?

_____

_____

_____

_____

_____

_____

_____

_____

_____

_____

_____

_____

_____

_____

_____

_____

_____

_____

_____

_____

_____

_____

_____

_____

_____

_____

_____

_____

_____

_____

_____

—*August*—

*I*s there any childhood fear that still haunts
you? How do you deal with this fear? _____

_____
_____
_____
_____
_____
_____
_____
_____
_____
_____
_____
_____
_____
_____
_____
_____
_____
_____
_____
_____
_____
_____

—August—

*H*ow do you enjoy helping people?
Share about a time when you helped someone in need.

—August—

If you could carve one more face on Mt. Rushmore, whose face would it be? Why?

In what ways are you like your mother? Like your father?

Looking back in life, what one thing would you have done differently? Why? _____

_____

_____

_____

_____

_____

_____

_____

_____

_____

_____

_____

_____

_____

_____

_____

_____

_____

_____

_____

_____

_____

_____

_____

Share some tips for a great vacation.

_____

_____

_____

_____

_____

_____

_____

_____

_____

_____

_____

_____

_____

_____

_____

_____

_____

_____

_____

_____

September

What lies behind
us and what lies before us
are tiny matters compared
to what lies within us.

Ralph Waldo Emerson

—September—

$\mathcal{D}$id you learn mechanics or woodworking
as a young person? How and when? What were
some of your most memorable projects?

_____
_____
_____
_____
_____
_____
_____
_____
_____
_____
_____
_____
_____
_____
_____
_____
_____
_____
_____
_____
_____
_____
_____
_____

—September—

Tell about a special outing you took with your dad. What makes this a poignant memory for you?

_____

*A*s a young person did you volunteer for work in church, community, or social services? Tell me about it.

_____
_____
_____
_____
_____
_____
_____
_____
_____
_____
_____
_____
_____
_____
_____
_____
_____
_____
_____
_____
_____
_____
_____
_____
_____
_____
_____
_____

When did you move away from home?
Describe where you lived and how you felt about it.

—September—

Tell me about some of your closest friends after you and Mom got married. What were some of the fun things you would do together? _____

._____
._____
._____
._____
._____
._____
._____
._____
._____
._____
._____
._____
._____
._____
._____
._____
._____
._____
._____
._____
._____
._____
._____
._____
._____
._____

What are your spiritual strengths? _____

How would you like to grow spiritually?

_____

_____
_____
_____
_____
_____
_____
_____
_____
_____
_____
_____
_____
_____
_____
_____
_____
_____
_____
_____
_____
_____
_____
_____
_____
_____
_____
_____
_____

What special talents did your parents nurture in you? How have you developed those talents?

_____

_____

_____

_____

_____

_____

_____

_____

_____

_____

_____

_____

_____

_____

_____

_____

_____

_____

_____

_____

_____

_____

What would you still like to learn to do? Why? _____

_____

_____

_____

_____

_____

_____

_____

_____

_____

_____

_____

_____

_____

_____

_____

_____

_____

_____

_____

_____

_____

_____

_____

_____

_____

_____

_____

_____

—September—

*What did you enjoy doing with your mom?
Share a special time with her.* _____

_____
_____
_____
_____
_____
_____
_____
_____
_____
_____
_____
_____
_____
_____
_____
_____
_____
_____
_____
_____
_____
_____
_____
_____
_____
_____
_____

—September—

*H*ow would you describe yourself:
tender-hearted or tough-minded?

*If you were to write a book about Mom, how would you title the book? The first few chapters?*_____

_____

_____

_____

_____

_____

_____

_____

_____

_____

_____

_____

_____

_____

_____

_____

_____

_____

_____

_____

_____

_____

_____

_____

How do you describe "success"?

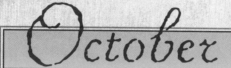

October

Life's journey is circular,
it appears. The years don't
carry us away from our fathers—
they return us to them.

—◦—

MICHEL MARRIOTT

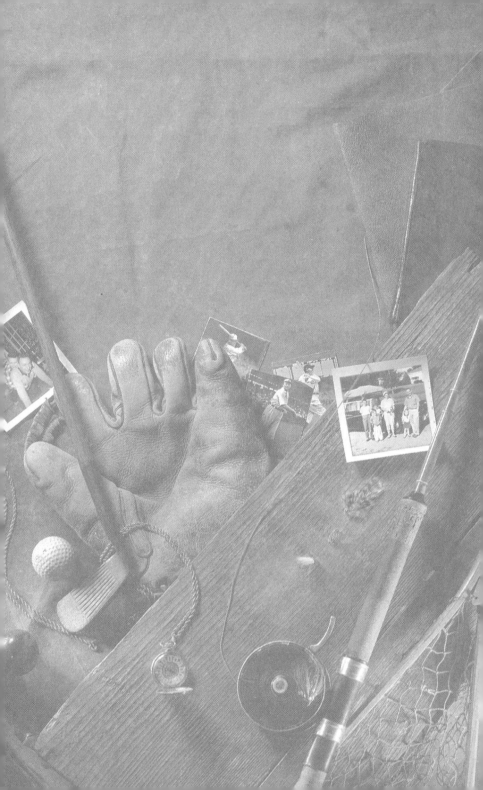

—*October*—

*W*hat spiritual legacy
would you like to leave for others?
Why is this important to you? _____

—October—

*S*hare a hilarious travel experience.

—October—

Do you have a favorite sports team?
Why is that one your favorite? none whatsoeva

—October—

What responsibilities did your parents require of you as a child? How did this affect your growth and development? How you raised your children? _____

164

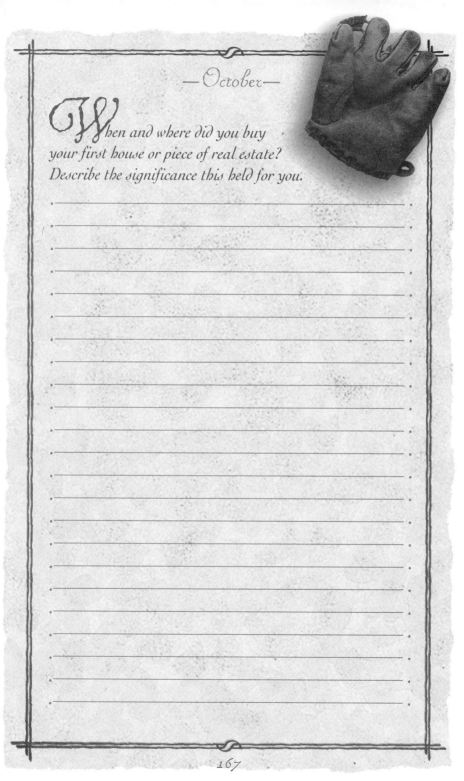

—October—

*W*hen and where did you buy
your first house or piece of real estate?
Describe the significance this held for you.

*W*hat is the strangest
thing you have ever seen? _____

_____

_____

_____

_____

_____

_____

_____

_____

_____

_____

_____

_____

_____

_____

_____

_____

_____

_____

_____

_____

_____

_____

_____

_____

_____

_____

Share some of your ideas on how to develop and maintain good physical health.

November

God calls each
generation to pass down
spiritual truth to the next.

———

DENNIS RAINEY

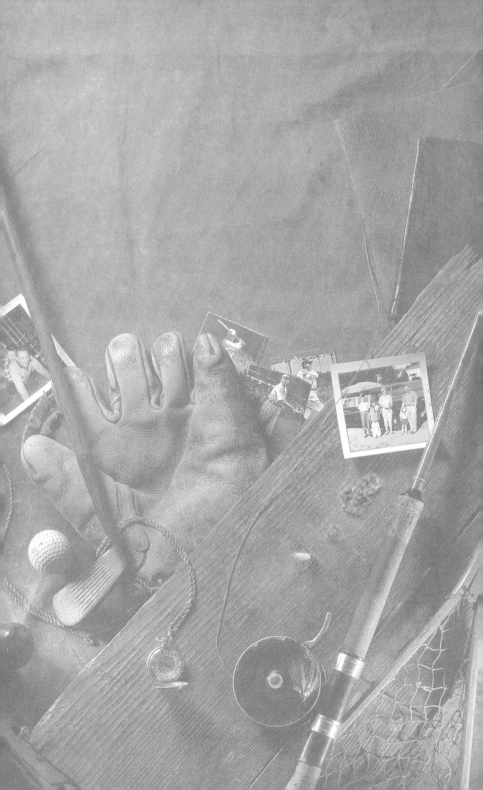

— November —

As a teenager, did you belong to a club or church youth group? Tell me about the individuals in the group who were most significant to you.

What is your most treasured possession and why? _____

_____

_____

_____

_____

_____

_____

_____

_____

_____

_____

_____

_____

_____

_____

_____

_____

_____

_____

_____

_____

_____

_____

_____

_____

_____

_____

—*November*—

*What Bible character
would you most like to meet? Why?*

_____

_____

_____

_____

_____

_____

_____

_____

_____

_____

_____

_____

_____

_____

_____

_____

_____

_____

_____

_____

_____

_____

_____

_____

— *November* —

What two people have made the greatest spiritual impact on your life? What made them so significant to you?

_____

_____

_____

_____

_____

_____

_____

_____

_____

_____

_____

_____

_____

_____

_____

_____

_____

_____

_____

_____

_____

_____

_____

_____

_____

_____

When you were a new father, what was your greatest fear? Your greatest joy?

—November—

What is your most vivid memory about my childhood? _____

_____

_____

_____

_____

_____

_____

_____

_____

_____

_____

_____

_____

_____

_____

_____

_____

_____

_____

_____

_____

_____

_____

_____

_____

_____

_____

_____

_____

What would you change about my childhood if you could?

Describe a fond Thanksgiving memory. What makes this special to you?

_____
_____
_____
_____
_____
_____
_____
_____
_____
_____
_____
_____
_____
_____
_____
_____
_____
_____
_____
_____
_____
_____
_____
_____

What are some things from your childhood that you are thankful for?

_____

_____
_____
_____
_____
_____
_____
_____
_____
_____
_____
_____
_____
_____
_____
_____
_____
_____
_____
_____
_____
_____
_____
_____
_____
_____
_____
_____

What childhood memory first comes to mind when you think about winter? How do you respond to that memory?

Describe the most interesting person you ever met. What were the qualities that made that individual so outstanding? _____

_____

_____

_____

_____

_____

_____

_____

_____

_____

_____

_____

_____

_____

_____

_____

_____

_____

_____

_____

_____

_____

_____

_____

_____

_____

_____

_____

_____

_____

—November—

What family customs or traditions would you like to pass on to your children and grandchildren. Why are they important to you? _____.

_____
_____
_____
_____
_____
_____
_____
_____
_____
_____
_____
_____
_____
_____
_____
_____
_____
_____
_____
_____
_____
_____
_____
_____

Tell me what four things
you would never leave behind
on a trip and explain why.

_____
_____
_____
_____
_____
_____
_____
_____
_____
_____
_____
_____
_____
_____
_____
_____
_____
_____

December

Those who loved you
and were helped by you will
remember you. So carve your name
on hearts and not on marble.

C. H. SPURGEON

Describe some Christmas traditions from your childhood and tell how they have influenced your life.

—December—

W

ere you ever in a Christmas program?
How did you respond to the experience? _____

_____
_____
_____
_____
_____
_____
_____
_____
_____
_____
_____
_____
_____
_____
_____
_____
_____
_____
_____
_____
_____
_____
_____
_____
_____

-December-

What is the best Christmas present you ever received? Why was that the best?

*T*ell about a memorable
Christmas visit with relatives. _____

_____
_____
_____
_____
_____
_____
_____
_____
_____
_____
_____
_____
_____
_____
_____
_____
_____
_____
_____
_____
_____
_____
_____
_____
_____
_____
_____
_____
_____

*W*hat is your favorite Christmas carol?
Why? _____

_____
_____
_____
_____
_____
_____
_____
_____
_____
_____
_____
_____
_____
_____
_____
_____
_____
_____
_____
_____
_____
_____
_____
_____

What would be the most wonderful gift you could receive? Why? _____

_____

_____

_____

_____

_____

_____

_____

_____

_____

_____

_____

_____

_____

_____

_____

_____

_____

_____

_____

_____

_____

_____

_____

_Tell me about a time when
God answered a specific prayer for you._

*What would you like to see happen
in the next ten years in your life? In the world?*

—December—

$\mathcal{A}$s you look back in life, name three of the most fantastic changes that have taken place in the world. How have these affected your life? _____.

_____
_____
_____
_____
_____
_____
_____
_____
_____
_____
_____
_____
_____
_____
_____
_____
_____
_____
_____
_____
_____
_____
_____

Where would you still like to go and what would you like to do once you got there?

_____

What is your favorite way to spend a rainy day?

_____
_____
_____
_____
_____
_____
_____
_____
_____
_____
_____
_____
_____
_____
_____
_____
_____
_____
_____
_____
_____
_____
_____
_____
_____
_____
_____
_____
_____
_____
_____

What word best describes your life? Explain why.

_____

_____

_____

_____

_____

_____

_____

_____

_____

_____

_____

_____

_____

_____

_____

_____

_____

_____

_____

_____

_____

_____

_____

_____

_____

What advice about life do you want others to remember?

_____
_____
_____
_____
_____
_____
_____
_____
_____
_____
_____
_____
_____
_____
_____
_____
_____
_____
_____
_____
_____
_____
_____

Notes